SUBWAY ART

Martha Cooper and Henry Chalfant

SUBWAY ART

Contents

Four-and-a-half top-to-bottom whole cars by Sizer, Paze, Midg, Fome, and Ence, 1982.

While thousands of kids are writing their names on every available surface in New York City, masterpieces such as appear on these pages are relatively rare. The "writers" face many obstacles in pursuit of their goal "to light up the line". They work in darkness, surrounded by dangerous machinery and live third rails, or balanced on the cross-ties of elevated tracks high above the street. Painting their names on the subway trains is illegal in New York City, and so the writers must be ready at any moment to dash down the tracks to safety if the police conduct a raid. In addition to such perils, they endure their irate parents' wrath at home and the attacks of hostile rivals in the streets.

All these risks do not guarantee success. A writer can never be certain that his work will ever be seen. New Yorkers who ride in subway trains daily are very likely to miss the best of the graffiti writers' work. Rivals cross out each other's names and the Transit Authority systematically cleans the trains with caustic solvents. Few "pieces" survive long; in fact, they are often destroyed even before leaving the yards. Therefore it is rare for

more than one or two undamaged graffiti masterpieces to be running in the entire transit system at any one time.

To get the photographs that are in this book, the authors spent thousands of hours stalking trains through the labyrinth of the transit system. For years they worked separately, unknown to one another, photographing these elusive works of art. Their methods were dissimilar, stemming as they did from very different points of view.

Marty, a photojournalist, took action shots of the writers while they pursued their vocation. She photographed their art on the trains as part of the whole urban environment. She found sites in the vicinity of the elevated tracks, where she could frame the trains as they passed by in a background of her own choosing. She spent many days in rubble-strewn lots or on rooftops of abandoned buildings in the South Bronx, waiting sometimes for three hours for a train to pass by in three seconds.

Henry began to photograph trains as a way of documenting this ephemeral art. An artist himself, he

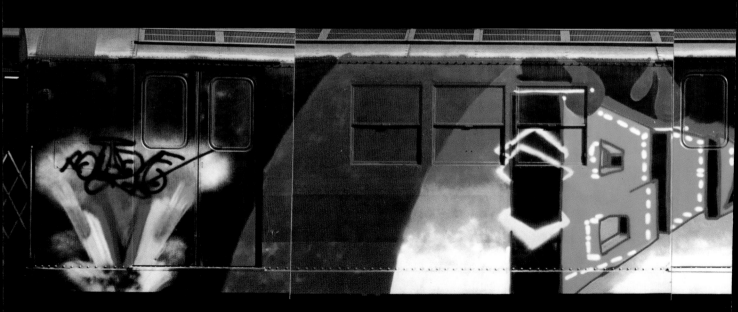

Blade, 1980.

focused his attention on the paintings, isolating them from their environment. A subway car is sixty feet long and it cannot be captured broadside with a normal 50mm lens when standing at a platform. When seen at an angle, the details of the farther end of the painting disappear. So Henry devised an unorthodox method of taking pictures: he stood on the above-ground station platforms, waiting for a freshly painted car to pull up on the opposite side to discharge and pick up passengers. When one appeared, he was able—with quick footwork—to shoot a series of four photos, each of a different section of the car. Later, he bought a motor drive for the camera, which enabled him to stand in one spot and shoot the series while the train was pulling out. In this way, over a period of seven years, he documented some five hundred paintings that no longer exist.

In the course of taking these pictures, the photographers were befriended by the graffiti writers. It was, in fact, they who introduced the photographers to each other. Marty and Henry discovered that their different approaches were complementary and that, by joining forces, they

could provide a better picture of graffiti work as an art form and as part of the life of New York City. Once the writers learned of this interest in their work, they kept the photographers informed whenever there were any new pieces running.

While knowing that a piece exists and where it might be running simplifies the task to some extent, getting the pictures can still be frustratingly difficult. It takes about four hours for a train to complete one round trip from 241st Street in the Bronx through Manhattan to New Lots Avenue in Brooklyn. But even waiting half a day does not bring guaranteed rewards. It is hard to predict which side the piece will be on; the car may not even leave the yard; hours can be spent patiently waiting for a piece, only for it to arrive just as a second train approaches from the other direction, obliterating the view. All this pales, however, when measured against the exhilaration felt at the successful capture of a "fresh burner".

8

Felix the Cat by Rasta.

Pluto by Mitch.

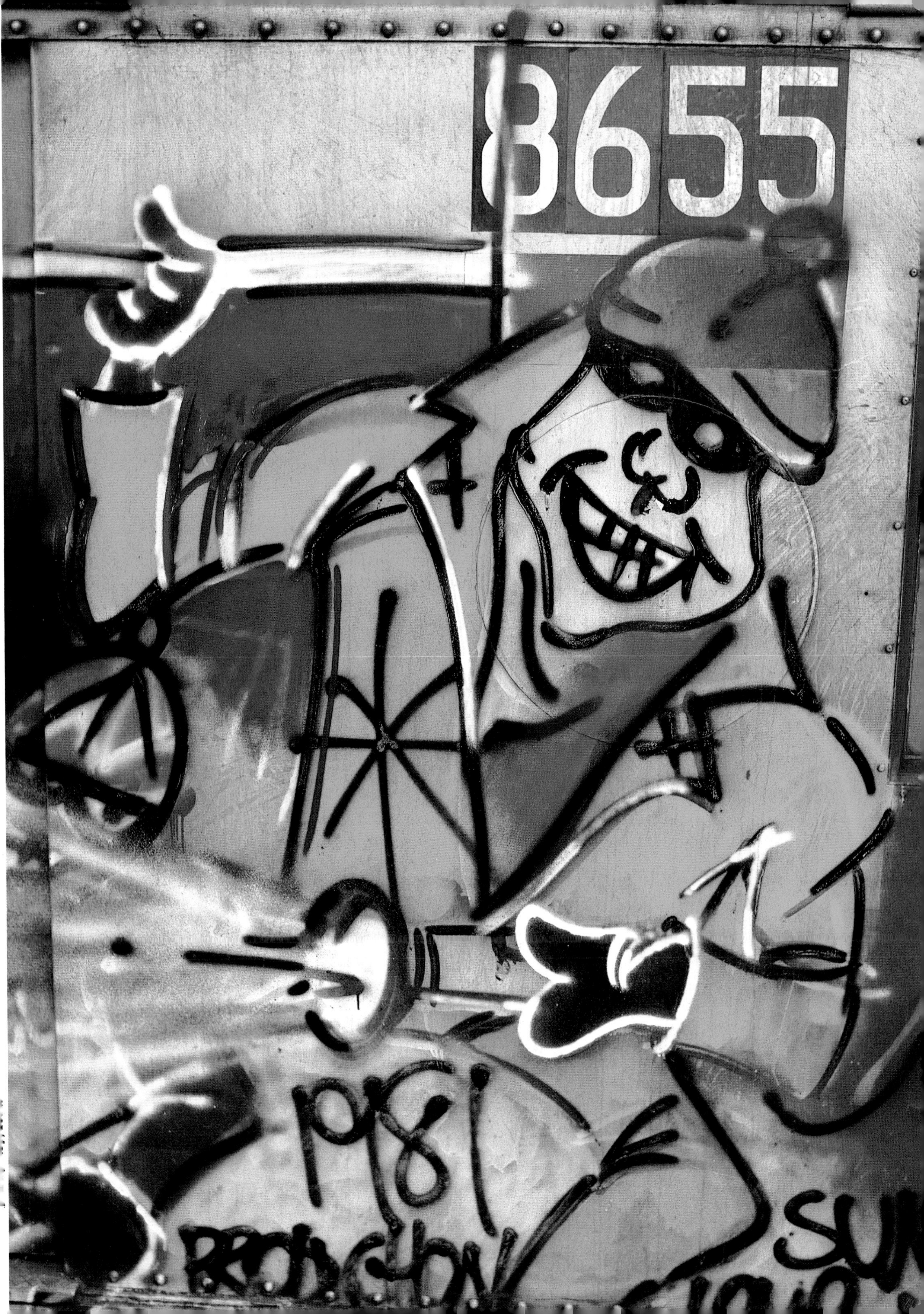
8655

Duro CIA, 1980.

Bus Eric, 1980.

Tags in the early 70s. Note Barbara and Eva 62.

14

mes   L.   37

'Taki 183' Spawns Pen Pals

Taki is a Manhattan teen-ager who writes his name and his street number everywhere he goes. He says it is something he just has to do.

His TAKI 183 appears in subway stations and inside subway cars all over the city, on walls along Broadway, at Kennedy International Airport, in New Jersey, Connecticut, upstate New York and other places.

He has spawned hundreds of imitators, including Joe 136, BARBARA 62, EEL 159, YANK 135 and LEO 136.

To remove such words, plus the obscenities and other graffiti in subway stations, it cost 80,000 man-hours, or about $300,000, in the last year, the Transit Authority estimates.

"I work, I pay taxes too and it doesn't harm anybody," Taki said in an interview, when told of the cost of removing the graffiti.

And he asked: "Why do they go after the little guy? Why not the campaign organizations that put stickers all over the subways at election time?"

Withholds Last Name

The 17-year-old recent high school graduate lives on 183d Street between Audubon and Amsterdam Avenues. He asked that his last name not be disclosed. Taki, he said, is a traditional Greek diminutive for Demetrius, his real first name.

"I don't feel like a celebrity normally," he said. "But the guys make me feel like one when they introduce me to someone. 'This is him,' they say. The guys knows who the first one was."

Taki said that when he began sneaking his name and street number onto ice cream trucks in the neighborhood early last summer, nobody else was writing similar graffiti.

"I didn't have a job then," he said, "and you pass the time, you know. I took the form from JULIO 204, but he was doing it for a couple of ve____ __n and he was

Taki, who began sneaking his name onto ice cream trucks last summer, has widened his field and won imitators. These marks are on door on 183d Street, where he lives.

The New York Times/Don Hogan Charles

taches drawn on advertising posters and various obscenities.

Officials s_i_ however,

teen-agers form all parts of the city, all races and religions and all econom_

History

The history of subway graffiti in New York is a brief one, and the phenomenon differs from all other kinds of graffiti, both past and present. In the 1960s, teenagers in New York began to write their names on neighborhood walls, but instead of their given names, they chose nicknames, creating a public identity for the street. Name graffiti initially had a territorial function. Gang members marked out their turf and local kids wrote for their friends or for their enemies.

Taki 183 was a youth who lived on 183rd Street in the Washington Heights section of Manhattan, but worked as a messenger traveling by subway to all five boroughs of the city. In his travels he wrote his name everywhere, including inside and outside trains and on every station. In 1971, a reporter tracked him down and interviewed him. The resulting article in *The New York Times* apparently struck a responsive chord in the hearts of Taki's contemporaries. Kids impressed by the public notoriety of a name appearing all over the city realized that the pride they felt in seeing their name up in the neighborhood could expand a hundredfold if it traveled beyond the narrow confines of the block. The competition for fame began in earnest as hundreds of youngsters, emulating Taki 183, began to "tag" trains and public buildings all over town. "Getting up" became a vocation. Kids whose names appeared the most frequently or in the most inaccessible places became folk heroes. Simultaneously, the widespread introduction of permanent markers and aerosol spray paint gave the graffiti writers greatly enhanced visibility.

As available space on walls and trains filled up, it was necessary to develop a style to make a name stand out from the rest. Kids began to practice variations on their names and to develop identifying logos which could be read at a glance. CONTINUED ON PAGE 17

Cover of a Leslie Charteris mystery, *The Saint Bids Diamonds*. These novels were the basis for a TV series which became popular with writers.

In 1973, *New York Magazine*, in a mock contest, gave "Taki Awards" for the best graffiti pieces. This piece by Spin won the award for Grand Design. Photo © Bill Ray.

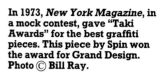

StayHigh 149 made a lasting impression on generations of graffiti writers with his innovative use of The Saint stick figure perched on his signature and smoking a joint. In this example, the joint is attached to the crosspiece of the letter "H". The halo and the smoking joint are the most commonly used symbols today in both "pieces" and "tags".

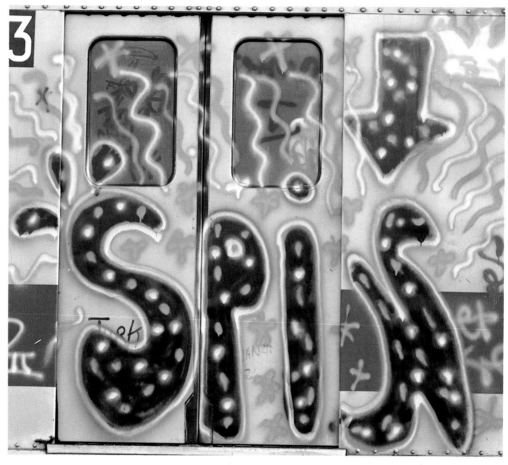

By the mid-70s, writers used highlights, overlapping letters, and three-dimensional effects in their pieces.

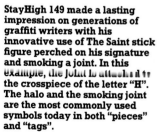

P. Nut, 1976.

A further development of graffiti is what the writers call "3-D", the illusion of depth. Writers began to use this technique extensively in the mid-70s. Here, the 3-D is distinguished from the face of the letters by imaginative use of color and design elements such as stars, flags, checkerboards, and dollar signs, all of which are called "designs" by the writers.

King 2, 1976.

In addition to style, writers began experimenting with size and color. They discovered that they could paint large areas quickly with spray paint and a new form, the "piece", was introduced. Short for masterpiece, early pieces were simply tags outlined with another color. As time went by, letters became larger and a variety of styles emerged simultaneously as writers from Brooklyn, the Bronx, and Manhattan intensified their efforts to keep up with the competition. The scale of the paintings grew until the entire side of the subway car, windows and all, was covered in the first "top-to-bottom whole car" painted in 1975.

Although two whole trains were completed, by Caine I in 1976 and by the Fabulous Five soon after, the top-to-bottom whole car remains the ultimate test of a writer's prowess. Style, however, continues to evolve rapidly, and the best of today's cars include complex compositions of "wildstyle" lettering with elaborate three-dimensional effects combined with cartoon characters.

Graffiti writing has already acquired a tradition, built on the contributions of several generations of writers. The upcoming artist finds himself in a situation in which the forms and conventions of his craft are established. The esthetic parameters within which he will work for the next few years as a practicing graffiti artist are fairly narrow. Major stylistic innovations are quickly adopted by other writers, who always remember the originators of those landmark breakthroughs: Hondo, the first top-to-bottom; Dead Leg, the first top-to-bottom with cloud, and so on. The names of the early pioneers, such as Phase 2, Stitch I, Barbara and Eva 62, and StayHigh 149, are legendary. Stories about them, their contemporaries, and their achievements comprise a body of graffiti folklore.

Old-style graffiti done by Smily and Ked, a couple of old-timers who did this anachronistic piece in 1980.

Carefully drawn drips have become part of the writer's repertoire, whereas drips resulting from the inept application of spray paint are to be avoided at all costs.

The New York City subway system links Manhattan with the Bronx, Queens, and Brooklyn.

Train Lines

The transit system connecting the far-flung boroughs of New York City is made up of three lines: the IRT (Interborough Rapid Transit), the BMT (Brooklyn Mass Transit), and the IND (Independent Subway System). These were originally separate private companies, but now operate under an umbrella organization, the MTA or Metropolitan Transportation Authority. Graffiti writers have a knowledge of the system which rivals that of any train buff or transit worker. They know the location of all the yards and lay-ups where trains are parked when not in use, and all the means of access, be they holes in the fence or out-of-the-way manhole covers that can afford a quick means of escape. CONTINUED ON PAGE 23

Airborne, 1981.

Noc, 1981.

Hell Iz for Children by Iz the Wiz, 1982, on a "flat" in the CC yard, the Bronx.

Writers classify the trains according to their desirability for painting. "Flats" are the best. These are the older trains, built around 1950, which have flat sides and a painted surface. Later models, such as "ridgies", so named for their corrugated stainless-steel flanks, are unsuitable for anything but "throw-ups", because the corrugated surface dominates any painted image and the stainless steel is easy to clean. Likewise, the "ding dongs", named for the bell that sounds when the doors open and close, are of stainless steel.

The Number 5 Lexington Avenue Express and its sister line, the Number 2 (the "Twos 'n Fives") have traditionally been the lines of choice of the best writers. Stretching from Dyre Avenue in the Bronx, where it runs above ground showing its graffiti-emblazoned sides to the world, the 5 traverses the length of Manhattan to end, finally, at Utica Avenue in Brooklyn. The round trip from Bronx to Brooklyn takes four hours.

The subway is a communications network on which the names and messages of graffiti writers circulate throughout the city. Kids begin watching trains early and they are thoroughly familiar with the names and styles of the "up writers" long before they attempt writing themselves. A youngster starting out finds a new community, focused on the subway, which brings together kids from all over the city. He gets a new name and a new identity in a group which has its own values and rules. He finds the particular subway stations where other writers congregate and where they form new alliances that transcend the old parochial neighborhood and traditional gang territory.

Rolieo Dien, 1982, on a No. 5 train at 180th Street station, the Bronx.

Overleaf: **CC yard, the Bronx.**

Adjectives such as bad, nasty, and vicious are used as boastful superlatives.

Greg, 1977.

Vocabulary

Writers have a specialized vocabulary, often metaphors for war and violence, such as "bomb", "hit", and "kill". The following glossary explains the terms most commonly used.

Bite   To copy another writer's style.
Bomb   Prolific painting or marking with ink.
Buff   Any means employed by the Transit Authority to remove graffiti from trains.
   To buff   To erase.
Burn   To beat the competition.
Burner   A well-done wildstyle window-down whole car; a burner is a winner.
Cap, fat or *skinny*   Interchangeable spray-can nozzles fitted to can to vary width of spray.
Crew   Loosely organized group of writers, also known as a *clique*.
Def   Really good (derived from "death").
Ding dong   Relatively new stainless-steel type of subway car, so named for the bell that rings just before the doors close.
Down   In, part of the group or action (e.g. "He's down with us").
Fade   To blend colors.
Flat   Older slab-sided type of subway car; the most suitable surface for painting.
Getting up   Successfully hitting a train.
Going over   One writer covering another writer's name with his own.
Hit   To tag up any surface with paint or ink.
Kill   To hit or bomb excessively.
King   The best with the most.
Lay-up   A siding where trains are parked overnight and on weekends.

Married couple   Two cars permanently attached, identified by their consecutive numbers.
Panel piece   A painting below the windows and between the doors of a subway car.
Piece   A painting, short for masterpiece.
   To piece   To paint graffiti.
Piece book   A writer's sketchbook.
Rack   To steal.
Ridgy   Subway car with corrugated, stainless-steel sides, unsuitable for graffiti.
Tag   A writer's signature with marker or spray paint.
Tagging up   Writing signature with marker or spray paint.
Throw-up   A name painted quickly with one layer of spray paint and an outline.
Top-to-bottom   A piece which extends from the top of the car to the bottom.
Toy   Inexperienced or incompetent writer.
Up   Describes a writer whose work appears regularly on the trains.
Wak   Substandard or incorrect (derived from "out of whack").
Wildstyle   A complicated construction of interlocking letters.
Window-down   A piece done below the windows.
Writer   Practitioner of the art of graffiti.

Seen, 1981.

Fame

"Getting fame" is the repeatedly stated goal of graffiti writers. Because there are so many thousands of writers in the city, to get fame an individual must stand out from the others. The competition is very intense. One can be "king" in several ways, such as King of the Line, or King of the Insides, or King of Style. A writer is judged by his mastery of painting and by the number of times he "gets up". All new pieces on the line are subjected to close scrutiny by self-appointed critics. Uppermost in the minds of the kids watching trains is always, "Who burned?" That is, which piece is the best? Winners are declared and the choice is hotly disputed.

Once a writer is "up", he finds himself on a treadmill. In order to get fame and to rise to the top of a multitude of competitors, he must get up over and over again. He is then rewarded by prestige and admiration—satisfactions he finds hard to part with. Once a writer stops for good, people soon forget about him, and new kings take his place.

Dez over Cap.

Cap over Shy.

Going over P Jay.

A throw-up which takes only minutes to execute will ruin a piece which may have taken eight hours of painstaking work to complete.

Going Over

The first rule of graffiti is that it is disrespectful to "go over" another writer's work. However, the competition is very intense, since there are so many writers and limited space on the trains. There have always been conventions for dealing with going over, including discussion, payment in kind (where the offended goes over the offender's name), and payment exacted in cans of paint or a punch on the jaw. Some writers go over others precisely to insult and challenge them. Blade says that he and Comet invented blockbuster letters "just to cover people".

Flying Eyeball **by Kid Panama.**

Flying Eyeball **by Seen.**

Biting

Writers prize originality above all else. Even though they borrow images from comics and TV, they scorn writers who copy from each other, accusing them of "biting". Seen and Kid Panama dispute who was the first to make use of this flying eyeball.

Two-man window-down wildstyle burner by Shy 147 and Kel, 1980.

Raul Wayne Sach, 1982.

a burner, 'cause like the colors wasn't bright . . . they wasn't outstanding. Like that Daze Skeme and Due . . . the Daze is like a burner, 'cause like the shit got def style, it got a def cloud, and the colors is bright. So it's a burner. It got everything that's supposed to be in a burner . . . the colors is def, the letters is def, and the def cloud and shit. A burner is connections, arrows. . . ."

Paint is accumulated over a long period, the writer's preferred colors being stocked up and stored at home.

Writers are thoroughly familiar with every color and brand of spray paint on the market, including vintage colors from the past, long since unavailable. Their favorite brands are Rustoleum, Red Devil, Wet Look, and Krylon.

Designing a piece.

Writers spend an afternoon working on their piece books and looking over photo albums of their pieces on trains.

Techniques

It takes a great deal of preparation to create a piece. Writers prepare sketches beforehand, carefully outlining the piece, drawing the characters, and noting the color scheme. The writer must accumulate the paint either by himself or by inviting friends who have paint to work with him. Buying paint is too expensive and is anyway not considered sporting, so the first task of an aspiring writer is to learn how to "rack" paint for his mentor.

Every hopeful young writer owns a sketchbook in which he practices piecing. In addition to his own work, the book contains pieces that other writers have done for him, which he can then use as models. And, of course, he spends many hours watching trains. According to Dez, a sixteen-year-old master, there is no easy way to learn the complicated wildstyle, and no substitute for time. Rather, the best way to learn is through recapitulating the entire history of graffiti art, from the simple to the complex: "When you're first starting and an up writer gives you style, it ain't easy to do it, so it be better to start from throw-ups to straight letters to semi-wildstyle to wildstyle. Then you can do anything you want after that. Rather than try to make your first piece be a burner and it looks wak, just work your way up. The trains ain't goin' nowhere."

One method used for perfecting style is photography. Writers always take pictures of their work, both as a record and as a learning device. There is really no other way to study a piece on the train properly, since it rarely stands still long enough or in the right places. Dondi says: "That's why we take pictures, 'cause when we take pictures we see our own mistakes and the next time we go we get better and better." CONTINUED ON PAGE 34

Nozzles from household products are fitted on spray-cans to vary the width of the spray. These are called "fat caps" or "skinny caps". The fat cap enables writers to paint large surfaces in a relatively short time.

Writers have acquired master keys to all the trains. These are duplicated and sold or traded to other writers.

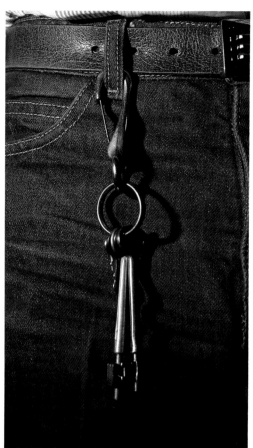

Kel outline with Cheech Wizard character in place of letter "E".

Kel piece on train.

Working sketches, called "original outlines", with the resulting pieces on the trains. Writers sometimes provide paint to a master in return for an outline.

Outline for 2 Many piece by Dondi.

2 Many piece completed.

T-Kid says: "The success of
every good writer is that they
get a good partner. One partner
gives the other partner style and
one does the fill-in. This is how a
lot of cars get done."

Once the train is selected, the writer lines up his colors
and sets to work. First he does an outline with a light color,
roughly blocking-out the letters. Then he fills it in and
adds a cloud or background scenery with characters.
Next he adds ornamental designs to the lettering. One
technique used is "fading", in which two colors are
blended into one another. Finally, he does the second
outline. This step, which defines the forms, is the most
crucial and it requires a very steady hand. It is difficult to
learn to control spray paint. The hand must move quickly
and with certainty when outlining, to avoid dripping. It
may take eight hours to do a whole car and require twenty
cans of spray paint.

A subway car is sixty feet long and twelve feet high. To do
a top-to-bottom in the yard, where there is no convenient
platform to stand on, a writer must climb up the side of the
car and hang on with one hand while painting with the
other; or, if his legs are long enough, he can straddle the
distance between two parked trains.

Going to the yards.

Entering a yard.

36

The source for Dondi's character, a Vaughn Bodé cartoon.

Children of the Grave Again, Part 3 by Dondi, 1980.

In the tunnels and yards, the trains are parked in parallel rows only a few feet apart. This makes it impossible for the artist to stand back and look at his work as a whole.

Graffiti writing is a public performance. A writer's reputation is on the line and the work of art done in the tunnel at night moves inexorably out into the public view the next day, exposing any drips, badly drawn characters, or inept lettering for the whole city to see. Often a writer will explain or apologize for mistakes on the work itself.

"You just don't know how badly I want to reach my hands on a can of spray and touch my big train set in my yard and feel the voltage running through them trains while I paint my ghetto name on that iron screen for my people of the state of NYC to see and wonder on the art of the ghettos and backstreets of our times." (Shy 147)

Seeing themselves as "bad" or "nasty" and as outlaws is one of the great attractions that graffiti writing has for adolescents. They need adventure. Mare, a sixteen-year-old student at the High School of Art and Design, who has been writing since he was twelve, says: "I see myself as a Tom Sawyer, wanting to seek adventure in every day I live. The last time I went piecing I didn't finish my piece, but I found a lot of adventure in this crazy journey."

Skeme reclining on the third rail in front of his piece.

Playing on a wrecked train.

LEO

RUST-OLEUM
STOPS RUST

SCRAME

caine
1

LOVE
TO
JAMIE
HAROLD

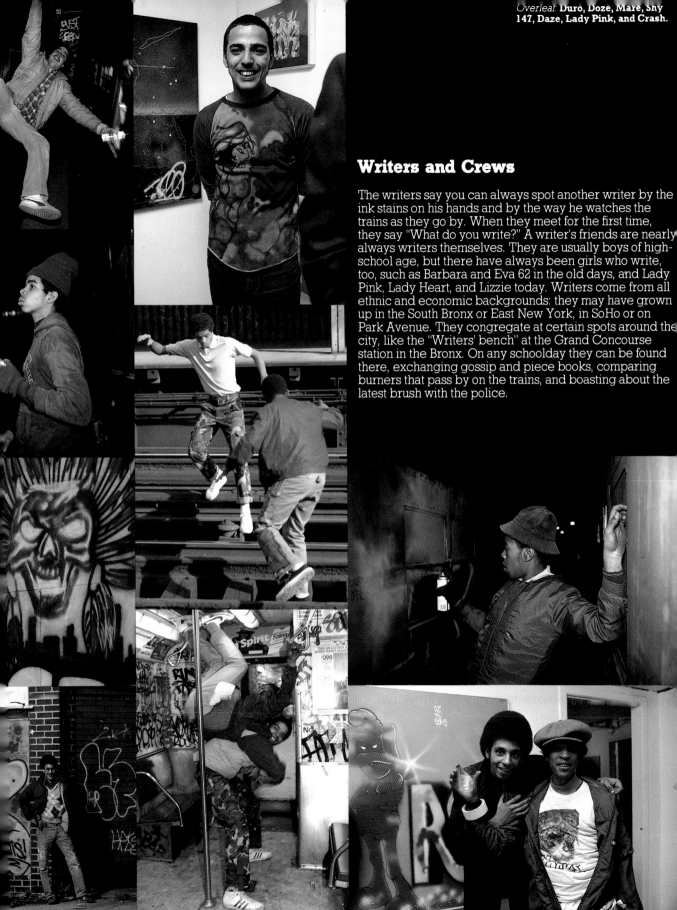

Overleaf: **Duro, Doze, Mare, Shy 147, Daze, Lady Pink, and Crash.**

Writers and Crews

The writers say you can always spot another writer by the ink stains on his hands and by the way he watches the trains as they go by. When they meet for the first time, they say "What do you write?" A writer's friends are nearly always writers themselves. They are usually boys of high-school age, but there have always been girls who write, too, such as Barbara and Eva 62 in the old days, and Lady Pink, Lady Heart, and Lizzie today. Writers come from all ethnic and economic backgrounds: they may have grown up in the South Bronx or East New York, in SoHo or on Park Avenue. They congregate at certain spots around the city, like the "Writers' bench" at the Grand Concourse station in the Bronx. On any schoolday they can be found there, exchanging gossip and piece books, comparing burners that pass by on the trains, and boasting about the latest brush with the police.

NAMES

The name is at the center of all graffiti art.
The writer usually drops his given name and
adopts a new one—a new identity. He can
make it up, inherit an established name from
an old writer, become part of a series such as
Take One, Take Five, and so on. Some names
are chosen for the esthetic possibilities in the
combination of letters they contain. Others
are chosen as puns, such as Ban II or Dis I.

Seen, 1981.

Seen.

Quik.

"When TNT crush you know it's us,
We are the crew the toys discuss.
We got the qualifications to turn the trains on,
That's what we be about.
We got the transit screamin' and shout,
We got the toys talkin' all about us,
'Cause we are the ones, we are the ones,
We are the ones that starts the funs."
(Agent)

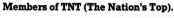

Members of TNT (The Nation's Top).

Crews

The initials such as OTB (Out Ta Bomb) or CIA (Crazy Inside Artists), which accompany the writers' names, stand for their crews. A crew, according to T-Kid, "is a unit of dudes who work together to achieve a goal: to get up and to go all city". Crews are made up of trusted friends, "a bunch of brothers that are down by street law with each other".

Loosely organized, writers can belong to more than one crew and be allied to many. Thus, a piece will often bear the initials of several crews. Because of the mobility of writers, crews transcend traditional neighborhood gang turf and draw upon the whole city for membership, often reflecting the interracial character of the graffiti world. The Vamp Squad, for instance, counts among its members kids of Peruvian, Scottish, Italian, African, Jordanian, Puerto Rican, and Albanian descent, and they live in Manhattan, Brooklyn, the Bronx, Staten Island, and Yonkers.

There is a strong sense of community within a crew and members will expel those writers who are only out for themselves. A popular crew will attract a lot of beginners who want to have the privilege of tagging up the name. Members jealously guard this privilege and will cross out the name of their crew where it has been used by someone not "down".

The Fabulous Five, 1976.

Trap with his mentor, Dez.

TPA (The Public Animals).

The Magnificent Team, 1977.

Kings

Graffiti writers often top their tags and pieces with a crown, symbolizing one of their goals—to be "king". This means to claim territorial rights over a certain line or other property by getting your name up on it more than anyone else. Two writers may race to be king of a line by seeing who can put up the most throw-ups, but the writers who are the most respected and widely acknowledged to be kings are invariably the best artists.

The greatest achievement of a writer is to be up a lot and to be at the same time a master of style. Still, an artist, no matter how good he is, cannot be king on the basis of only a few beautiful cars. He must succeed over and over again in order to maintain his position.

"A king is a writer that everyone either wants to write with or fight with" (Iz the Wiz).

Delta, 1982.

I ONCED
LOVED

Love Sick ☆
Sick
BOMBER!

Hand of Doom by Seen, 1980.

Blade, 1980.

Children of the Grave Return, Part 2 by Dondi, 1980.

Style Wars by Noc, 1981.

Style

"Style" is a very concrete idea among writers. It is form, the shapes of the letters, and how they connect. There are various categories of style, ranging from the old, simple bubble letters or peppermint-stick letters to the highly evolved and complex wildstyle, an energetic interlocking construction of letters with arrows and other forms that signify movement and direction.

Sab Kaze, 1982.

Styles vary from writer to writer, from crew to crew, and from line to line. The 6 line, for example, had a style which could be attributed to the influence of one outstanding writer, Seen. Seen had a profound impact upon a score of younger writers, not only members of his crew (United Artists) but also many others for whom he was simply the king.

Seen trained several young apprentices. He taught them the yard, the technique, and let them help him with the simpler tasks, such as filling in the rough outline. Sometimes they put up their own pieces under his guidance and with his help on the more difficult tasks, such as the final outline. In the exchange, the younger

CONTINUED ON PAGE 70

Blade tag.

Zephyr of Mafia crew.

Futura 2000, 1973.

Futura 2000, 1983.

TAGGING

The tag is a stylized personal signature. Kids work hard at perfecting their tags before making them public, and in tagging they confront for the first time the need to have style. Tagging is done with either marker or spray paint.

Most writers keep the same style of tag for their entire writing career: it becomes their identifying logo and is instantly recognizable to other writers. Futura, however, has updated his logo in keeping with his new image as a fine artist. His old tag included SA with a smoking joint, the sign for Soul Artists, his former crew.

Lady Pink with freshly painted tag.

THROW-UPS

The throw-up is a name painted quickly with one layer of spray paint and an outline. Writers use throw-ups when quantity and speed are more important than quality, for instance, when two rivals are vying for control of a line.

Throw-up by Quik, 1982.

Scab II by Skeme, 1981.

PANEL PIECES

In a window-down panel piece, one name extends from the base of the window to the bottom of the car and fills the width of the panel between the doors.

Work by Rasta, 1981.

WINDOW-DOWN WHOLE CAR

A window-down whole car consists of two or three names below the windows and extending the length of the subway car. These pieces can be in any of three or four current styles, but when more than one artist is involved, the collaborators try to maintain stylistic harmony with one another. In fact, one artist often supplies the sketches for the others, thus ensuring a unity of style. The piece may float on a cloud or stand alone. Writers say that the cloud was invented to clean up the background for the piece, so that the observer is not distracted by the ghost images from past pieces still visible on the car.

writers got their name up and learned their skills, while Seen had more pieces running, his style became more widespread, and his hegemony on the line grew. Masters like Dondi or Tracy 168, preeminent on other lines, have had a similar influence on younger writers, creating schools of followers.

As Tracy 168, an old-timer, explains it: "I was teaching T-Kid. It was easy since I had the Ts. I gave him a couple of letters and styles and the rest he had to learn himself. I showed him loops and shit. He went out there and brought it out, plus added on whatever he saw. So I taught him and he was the best on the line, and at the same time I could sit home and still be king of the line."

Many writers dislike wildstyle lettering because it is difficult to read. For others, the illegibility reinforces their sense of having a secret society, inaccessible to outsiders. Dondi says that, when he writes for other writers, he uses

wildstyle, and when he writes for the public, he uses
straight letters.

A writer will therefore often make a piece deliberately
hard to read. There is pressure on him to make his style
more complex, partly to enhance his reputation as a
virtuoso and partly to discourage other writers from
"biting" or stealing it. "I throw 'em off with the camouflage.
That way they can't bite my style", says Kase 2, widely
acknowledged "king of style".

"Wildstyle was the coordinate style and then computer.
That's what I brought out. Nobody else can get down with
it 'cause it's too fifth-dimensional. I call it the fifth-
dimensional step parallel staircase, 'cause it's like
computer style in a step-formulated way. It's just sectioned
off the way I want. Like if I take a knife and cut it, and slice,
you know, I'll slice it to my own section and I'll call it
computer style."

Kase 2.

TOP-TO-BOTTOM

A top-to-bottom is a piece which extends the whole height of the car, from the top to the bottom, but not necessarily the whole length.

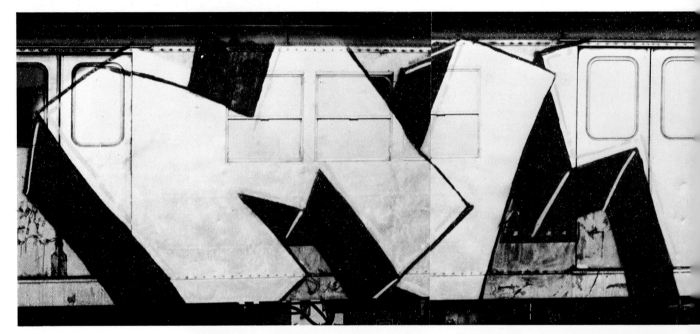

Mitch 77, 1981.

Code by Duro, 1980.

Iz the Wiz, 1982.

Mad, 1982.

TOP-TO-BOTTOM WHOLE CAR

A top-to-bottom whole car covers the entire side of the car, windows and all. Some writers will only do top-to-bottom whole cars, disdaining anything less complete. Others, particularly during periods when the Transit Authority is vigilant, feel that to cover the windows is a waste of time, since these are the first part of the car to be cleaned, and usually with a solvent which drips down, streaking the piece below. Window-downs last longer, but the top-to-bottom whole car is the graffiti writer's finest achievement. It is here that he displays his virtuosity, creating landscapes, fantasy worlds, and visions of heaven and hell.

Seen Mitch, 1980.

Trap Dez Daze, 1983.

Overleaf: ***Tuff City*** **by Skeme and Phase 2, 1982, at 174th Street, South Bronx.**

TOP-TO-BOTTOM WHOLE CAR WITH CHARACTERS

A top-to-bottom whole car with character by Mad and Seen, who are brothers. Characters frequently act as heralds, their gestures drawing attention to the name.

Mad Seen, 1980.

Seen P Jay, 1980.

Characters

While some writers invent their characters, most are content to lift them from the fields of the mass media and American popular culture. They build their own iconography by selecting images from comics, TV, and advertising, and reassembling them in new contexts. Often the character expresses the writer's own self-image.

In spite of the extensive borrowing, writers are inventive in the applications to which they put these borrowed forms in their overall designs. They admire originality more than any other characteristic in their colleagues' artwork. As Tracy 168 puts it: "When you got enough balls to waste paint and try something new, that's when you're a writer!"

Mitch, 1980.

Dust Sin, 1982.

Sweet Cousin Cocaine by Kid
Panama, 1981.

Overleaf: **Son 1 Rem, 1983, at
125th Street and Broadway,
Harlem.**

**Donkey Kong and Mario
characters by Son 1 and Rem,
1983.**

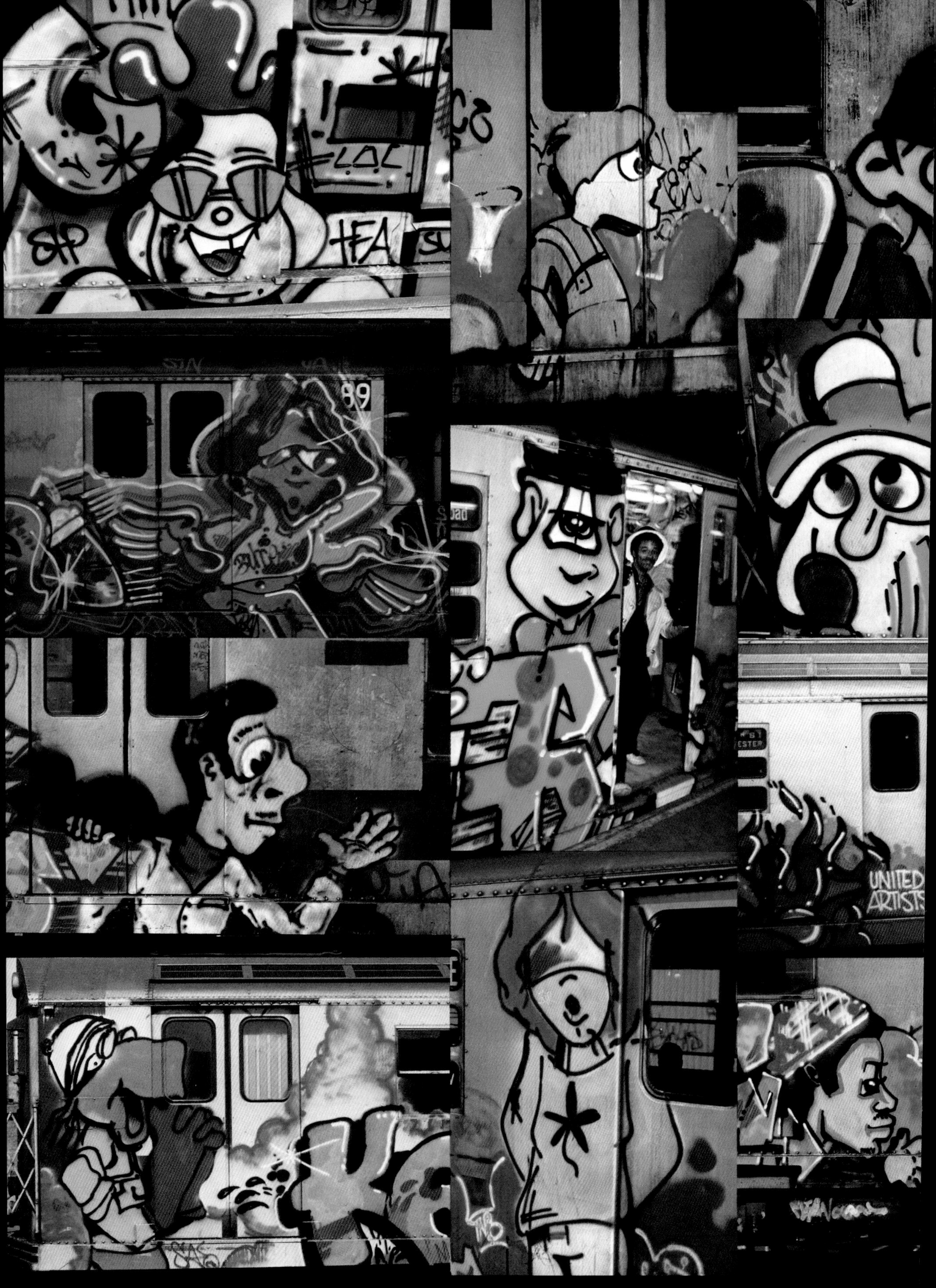
UNITED
ARTISTS

Sometimes characters are used in place of letters.

Sonic Bad, 1981.

Disco, 1981.

T-Kid, 1980.

Quik, 1981.

Spin, 1982.

Blade and Dolores.

Love Stinks by Zephyr.

Dedication by Zephyr: "For the ladies in my life who save my graffiti drenched brain from cracking up."

Blade and Dolores by Blade, 1978.

Blade and Dolores by Blade, 1981.

Dedications

Writers enjoy seeing their names travel around town, and at times they let their friends or families share in this by putting their names up too. Thus, there are many dedications on the trains honoring sweethearts and mothers.

Writers also use the trains as a public forum, where they can make philosophical or political statements.

91

Duster and Lizzie.

Duster Lizzie, 1982, crossing the Bronx River at Whitlock Avenue.

Deli, 1981.

Mom by Seen.

Mom by Seen. Photo by Seen.

177 Street
Parkchester

Brooklyn Bridge
Manhattan

6 Lex Av Local
Pelham Exp

93

Mom **by Kid Panama.**

Mom **by Lee.**

Lee with his Mom.

Eulogy to John Lennon and
deceased rock stars by Lady
Pink and Iz the Wiz, 1981.

94

Stop the Bomb by Lee, 1979.

Spin's response to Mayor Koch's
anti-graffiti campaign, 1982.

Overleaf: *Happy Holiday* by
Richie (Seen) and Jason, 1982, at
174th Street, South Bronx.

95

Skeme, 1982.

Lee, 1979.

98

The boys in blue.

Opposition

There is opposition to the writers, particularly among public officials who appear to have lost control over the subways. The police department has created special squads of detectives who conduct raids in the yards and tunnels to catch writers. These detectives maintain extensive dossiers on the writers and sometimes press captured toys into service as informers. Doubtless, this elaborate cops and robbers game contributes to one important incentive for writing graffiti: to enhance the prestige of the writer in the eyes of his peers.

Sherlock by Lee, 1978.

The Buff

In its ten-year fight against graffiti, the MTA has tried a number of defenses, but the one most dreaded by writers is the chemical wash or the "buff". Blade will never forget how, in the span of a few weeks in 1978, he lost dozens of his whole cars by this means.

The buff uses a strong chemical paint solvent, developed especially to remove graffiti. Trains are driven under a shower of remover and washed off after standing for a few minutes. Although this method uses fifty-five gallons of chemical per train, the technique is imperfect for all but the newest models. On the older types, which have the flat painting surface preferred by writers, the chemical only partially removes the piece. Cleaning trains therefore often makes them messier than before and is an invitation for other writers to go over the freshly buffed piece.

Fuck the Buff by Seen, 1980.

Graffiti Died by Seen, 1982.

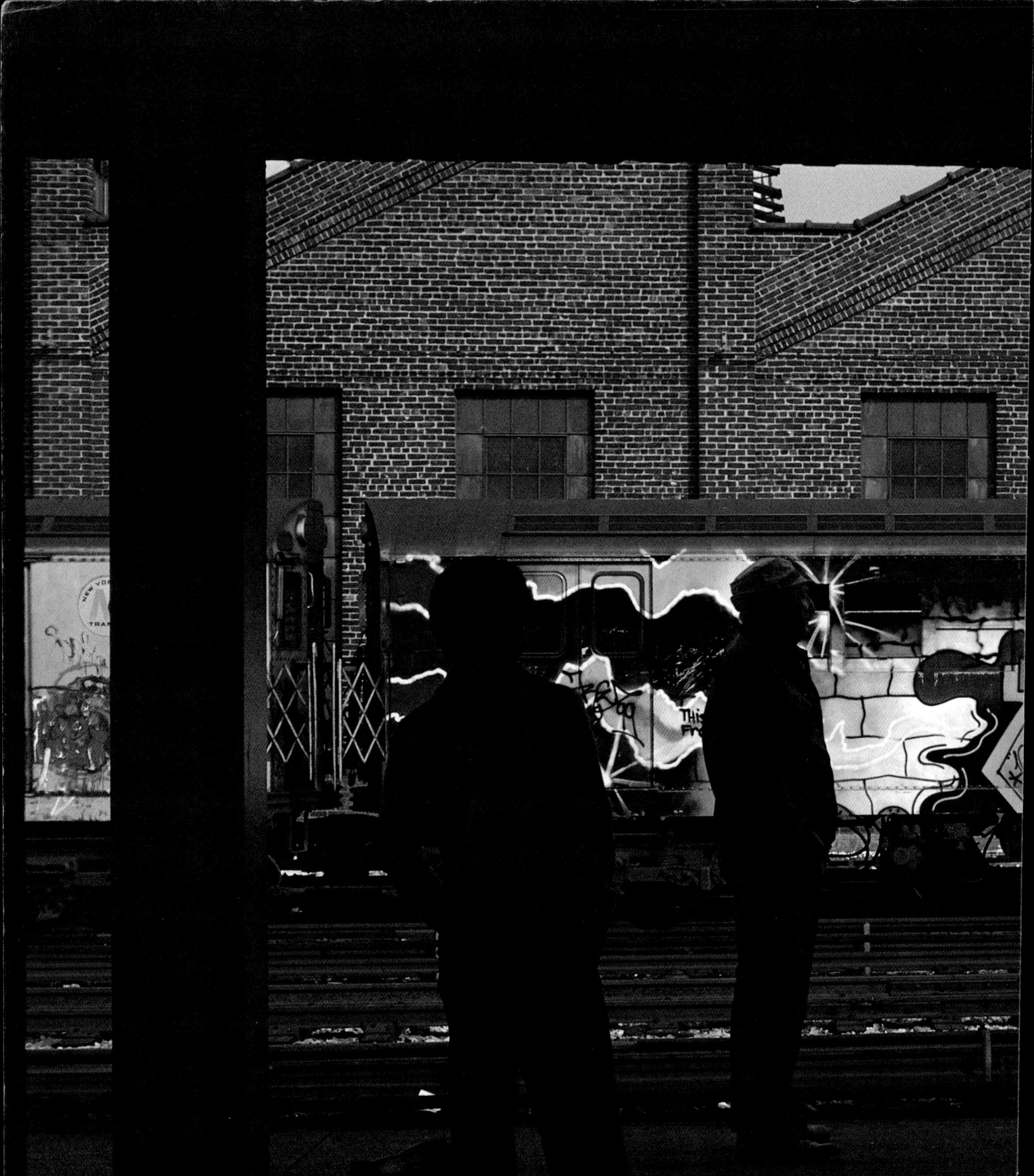

THERE WAS ONCE A TIME
WHEN THE LEXINGTON WAS A BEAUTIFUL LINE
WHEN CHILDREN OF THE GHETTO EXPRESSED
WITH ART, NOT WITH CRIME. BUT THEN AS
EVOLUTION PAST THE TRANSITS BUFFING DID ITS
BLAST. AND NOW THE TRAINS LOOK LIKE RUSTED
TRASH. NOW WE WONDER IF GRAFFITTI WILL
EVER LAST...????????

Epitaph by Lee, 1980.